FOREST PRIMEVAL

VIEVEE FRANCIS

FOREST PRIMEVAL

Poems

TRIQUARTERLY BOOKS/NORTHWESTERN UNIVERSITY PRESS

EVANSTON, ILLINOIS

TriQuarterly Books
Northwestern University Press
www.nupress.northwestern.edu

Printed in the United States of America

10   9   8   7   6   5   4   3   2   1

Library of Congress Cataloging-in-Publication Data
Francis, Vievee, author.
   Forest primeval : poems / Vievee Francis.
      pages cm
   ISBN 978-0-8101-3243-6 (pbk. : alk. paper) — ISBN 978-0-8101-3244-3 (ebook)
   I. Title.
   PS3606.R3653F67 2015
   811.6—dc23

                                                                        2015025256

The paper used in this publication meets the minimum requirements of the American National Standard for Information Sciences—Permanence of Paper for Printed Library Materials, ANSI Z39.48–1992.

For Matthew Olzmann

Contents

FOREST PRIMEVAL

ANOTHER ANTIPASTORAL

I want to put down what the mountain has awakened.

My mouthful of grass.
My curious tale. I want to stand still but find myself moved patch by patch.
There's a bleat in my throat. Words fail me here. Can you understand? I sink to
my knees tired or not. I now know the ragweed from the goldenrod, and the
    blinding
beauty of green. Don't you see? I am shedding my skins. I am a paper hive,
    a wolf spider,
the creeping ivy, the ache of a birch, a heifer, a doe. I have fallen from my dream
of progress: the clear-cut glass, the potted and balconied tree, the lemon-waxed
wood over a marbled pillar, into my own nocturne. The lullabies I had forgotten.
How could I know what slept inside? What would rend my fantasies to cud and up
from this belly's wet straw-strewn field—

                                                    these soundings.

WHITE MOUNTAIN

There's a wind here so strong it shakes this stone house.
A howl from pain and cold, a particular anguish—
not a foot in a trap, but a foot in a trap and the snow
getting deeper. I look out under the leafless beech,
which I'd take for dead if I didn't believe in spring's coming.
I walk around the property thinking I might happen upon
the source of the sound. How could that cry be wind alone?
Something has snapped in two. Something has been lost
that won't return in this life. I want to find the source.
I'm stumbling in a thin coat that flaps at my sides. It seems
as if I might ride the beast that haunts me if I could just let go.
Let it take me up easily as this gale is lifting me now.

into wild darkness and wild darkness
        descending
                —Michael Collier, "Keats and Francesca"

. . . and in accents disconsolate answers the wail of the forest.
                —Henry Wadsworth Longfellow, *Evangeline: A Tale of Acadie*

I

List to a Tale of Love in Acadie, / home of the happy.
> —Henry Wadsworth Longfellow, *Evangeline: A Tale of Acadie*

HAPPY?

I would not say so. Rather, settled
in *this* moment where no axe falls.

And one might wonder why
not *happy* in such an idyllic place—

with more trees than might be named
and the blooms ever blooming

in a heat seemingly ceaseless
as the red-throated woodpeckers,

as the tree frogs mating endlessly
on the same limbs a black bear might

loll from, indolent and berry-full.
You have heard me say, *Nature*

will have its way. That we build
only way stations. I was proud.

I thought I understood, but
now I have come to this ridge,

which wrests its toll: my sleep
grows longer, my dreams follow

into my days. I have begun to name
the birds by their feathering, their calls

and clamor: nightjar, flicker, plover, shrike.
Before the mountain I knew the incinerated

cities. I knew another South. But that
was before I was another. The one

I am becoming as roots reclaim
this soil, as what is felled takes on

a form it could not have imagined,
whose seeds had always rested below

like a sorrow of banjoes.

ALTRUISM

Given the torch, given the Wild Turkey, given
the reason, given the moment, given away,
given another reason, given the window
that frames the night's cool,
given the shots and the stars in their black wraps,
given that party (you know the one) with smoke
and champagne and paintings you wanted to sink
inside of, given the way you—

                                        given hunger,
so many kinds of hunger, given the restaurants,
the cafés, the bistros and diners where all
the loud beauties flaunt their wares, where all
that red-tipped fury comes in a tight dress, given that
kind of sophistication, the kind that craves its own
reflection and finds it, given (and it is a given) your desire
as an abyss none can fill or fathom, given the received
needs of men and women to be pleased and please,
given the construction of a bird's nest of pain, a bundle
of found objects and thin limbs, give me something
else.

        Give me the fruit I may leave *my* mark upon
or flesh (willing enough), but something, something
besides lip and the language of loss. Give me the pleasure
of knowing the giving matters to more than the receiver,
and given such knowledge give me faith, or denial, or
truth enough to manage this
truth such as it is.

CRACKS ALONG THE OUTER BANKS

Then, I had imagined only the scuffle of turtles on the island's bed of sand,
their brown flippers and mottled armor (that slightly repulses
in glossed pictures) moving determinedly. I followed my father in manic desire
to examine the natural world; rather, depictions of it.

So when he found the porn stash behind my bed I did not deny it.

I was a child but not a liar. I could not understand what was counterintuitive.

He said *wrong* and I said *why* and continued

my explorations by text just like a little marten with her mouth open

and her eyes scanning the horizon for the promise of more, until

a body at last opened its mysteries to me shortly after I became aware

of my own. Now, I too have lain on the sand belly down

having fought my way away from the interminable suck of the current

even as I long to inhabit those deeper waters, to stand on the edge

of another shelf from which I might fall into that pressured abyss, to be

held and held tighter, tighter until my own pied shell relents.

EMANCIPATION

after Kara Walker

The starlings exploded from your chest.
How many had you swallowed? How many?
A volary of the body, one then
another, every sorrow winged and seeking
an invitation, took its place in your breast, crowded
along the lung's limbs. There was no room, but
they kept coming. You couldn't keep your mouth shut,
so more, then more sought that grotto, craned throats
of despair bent on entering. And what was it they wanted?
What drew such slights, small remarks, unintelligible
suspicions, slaps, *leurs petits besoins*, harbingers?
Birds not of prey but pity. Pity your shrieking head. Pity
your pecked liver, useless spleen. Every insult you took
in. No room for love, *O cher nigaud*, the dandered windows,
the butted floor of you, on and in they flew
bird by bird until,
                    until—
until, who could have held on to such things? Who?
I don't blame them for wanting out. I don't blame them.
Once inside they couldn't keep. You fought to keep it down.
You finally closed the gate, pressed your lips together. *Mine*,
you said. *Mine*. And what could stand that? Pity
love's tick-riddled feathers. Its stricken feet. What was left
to do but flee? So out they burst, yellow billed
from your dark coop
                    to mine.

TAKING IT

for Gabby and Jen

I never remember the knuckles, though
his hand was bare, though their hands were bare.
I remember the impressions left on *this* skin, the
wilting and the welting. I don't remember the sound,
not one smack. I remember the falls, myself falling
to the floor or sidewalk, or against the brick wall
my head met after a push. There were many pushes.
Girls pushed but I punched. Pulled one
down by the hair and kneed her as my head bled.
Girls didn't punch until high school. I had always
punched. *What kind of girl are you?*
The kind who wants to live, I said, and I did want to
until I didn't anymore. But I wanted the leaving
to be on my terms, so I hit my father back.
He owned me like any good, country father. He
waited for a husband to tame what he couldn't corral,
to throw a rope like fingers 'round a neck.
When I missed a boy, fingerholds—I remember those,
and me making a fist wrongly, and punching
and I didn't mean to miss but to hit the line below the belly,
the beltline. W—— broke me in the snow
my first year North. I'm still afraid to say his name.
I wore shoes too thin for the weather (who had ever seen
such snow?) and had a Georgia lilt, like molasses
on a sore throat, sugared, raw, and he hated the sound of it.
He was black and I was black and I was so happy
to be in Detroit, and he aimed for my heart-
shaped mouth, my gapped teeth, my too-sweet tongue.

I felt the juvenile weight of him above me like snow after dark
falling steady and hard. *I'm gone teach you to talk reg'lar,*
and I stopped speaking at all. I kept my swollen mouth shut,
and a straight razor in my math book, and dreamt of a bat
cracking against his chest. A woman like me
with soft hands, not hands of the field, but
hands meant to stroke and soothe, needs a weapon,
so I studied *The Art of War* and watched boxing, and
where else was all this rage to go? Is this too dramatic?
Find another story. Find a lie. In love, body after body
fell beneath my own, though my own was broken,
and I made love like a sea creature, fluid as if boneless,
though my bones would rattle if not for the fat I cherish.
Wouldn't you? And I grew to love the heavyweights,
myself with one in the ring. Imagine him punching
me, and punching me again, saying *I'm sorry, so sorry,*
to have to love you this way.

A FLIGHT OF SWIFTLETS MADE THEIR WAY IN

and settled along my cage—

so expectantly beautiful,
their swerve, I wanted to touch
them, to take their tiny frames
    and snap their necks.
Tell me you haven't felt that way.
Tell me
you haven't wanted to stifle what hovers
dumb before your heart?
I hollowed myself into a cave
for others. I opened wide as a tomb
from which the stone has been rolled and
in they flew to the emptiness of me,
where they made themselves a home,
nested lickety-split in my walls.
    I have never been whole,
so there was room. Now inside
I am less inclined to hurt them but
consider taking flight myself, wind-borne
from some vertiginous place, why not? With so many
wings within beating beating
                  beatingbeating
           beatingbeating   beating
               beating

THE ACCOUNTANT

I keep a ledger because I want to know the bend
of the tale. There's truth not in but *under* the details
like dirt beneath a rouged thumbnail, or
flesh under fingertips blued by ink and sugar.
There are secrets that won't free you. Secrets
without purpose. I'm keeping a record so it gets told
right, the story—the *personal narrative* if that helps.
I'm allowing that it doesn't always get better,
isn't always "alright." A happy ending may mean
I'll meet you farther along . . . or, could be
you'll never see me again. Don't pretend.
Why the long face?
You don't need a sin for a savior. Get up,
look at the flaw in this counterpane.
Allow me to tug the thread until we are both bare,
to run my finger down the column. Isn't that better?
Freed of your scholarship? Of your reliance on theories
of light? That pacifier
like a cloud in the mouth of God.
                            Won't it feel good to feel
as if the sky were yours alone "naked as a blue jay"?
"as the day you were born"?

APPROACHING FIFTY

for John
(Hamtramck, Michigan)

With our down-turned mouths, and trenches
now on either side, evidence of our disappointments.
Look at the nests by the eyes—we were so easily amused,
(what else was there to be), and nurtured (if reluctantly)
by those who insisted upon our goodness. Ah, morality.
Did you buy it? I didn't. Ethics, sure, sure one needs those,
but I value only the morals of furrows. Look at my brow,
I know what I know. We are sinners, you and I, but
I can live with that. I won't speak for you,
my friend. What are we doing? With such good (or
good enough) lives and our not deserving a bit of it but
having earned it. See how easy it is to laugh at this age.
So much is funny after so many tears. You get sentimental
and it leads to truth because we are reaching that time when
we don't give a damn about other eyes upon us. I'm glad
you are here even if you weren't there. You were doing
whatever it was men do, and I was meant to survive you and
then some. Meant to and did and isn't that why you're here?
It's good to see what survives us, how we are then freed
to move away, on, but never back. I told you I wasn't "nice."
Nice women don't get this far. And you, well,
you were worse, but look at me becoming nostalgic.
We're here to discuss the turn of years over a coffee. To
note how much we forgive each other's fallen faces.

SHALL WE GATHER & WHAT

(Detroit, Michigan)

Up from the heatless church come the eloquent tambourines

of the congregants, the gloved handclaps, shouts through gelid air: *I believe,*

Preach, yes Sir . . . Up comes the director, a model for the less evolved,
a guide

through a forest of broken lamps and bullet-riddled siding (though who would guess

in his righteous character he craves what any sinner might crave, just

as the marsupial craves the opiate of night, its eyes enlarged for viewing—

                              something to assuage his jones). *Jesus.*

Up from the pews one cry in varied timbers: *Help us, Lord,* to be more like you,

impervious or at least unafraid.

          Behind the parking lot a pit lolls with its owner contemplating

what door to jimmy while the preacher calls out, *Let the doors of the church be opened,*
and all stand to sing wide an aperture through
                              which few enter whole

and none can afford to leave. Think of the cost:

The glass shattered beyond repair

                                                        and no dust broom.

The child shot in the head and no heaven to right the wrong.

that gathered there along his arms,
upon the invitation of a slender limb.
And not oblivious to human violence
perhaps needed rest or needed to offer
the succor of presence, despite the
stiff collar of their feathers, despite
each one being no less the children
of a father who claimed an upper realm.

It is not true they pecked his eyes. Nor
did they consider his wounds
their own. They were neither irreverent
nor quiet. They spoke in the tongues
they knew. They cawed full voiced
and would have released him from his
bindings had their beaks held the power
and had there been time in that place.

Like them, I have sought to comfort and
so be comforted. Like them
I have seen the failure of miracles when
they were most needed. Like Him, I
have called upon those so unlike myself
when my father failed to answer.

FALLEN

But I was never the light of my father's eyes, or any
other *brother*'s (that deep-husked choir), so there
was no height from which to fall. I began here
                                in the proverbial bottom:
undertow, base from which one may rise but briefly,
like the failing horse knowing it must now race, must
tear out of its rusted gate, must further tear
the pleuritic lining of its lungs, let its tongue loll
                ugly from the side
of its mouth. Have you seen such a thing?
Its brown coat salted with sweat as it lunges
forward and lunges again, forcing its measure
not up but out, knowing its ankles could fold
under such weight, its nose opened
into another being, sucking and snorting
the only thing it takes within that does not judge it,
the air. The sweet, sweet air
as it makes its way around a curve that might kill it,
that assuredly will kill it. Do you see me there?
Of course not.
                I'm over here. Here,
in *this* hollow running for my low life. O Father,
for the rub of a hand over my back. O Brothers,
for the gold-leaf wreath that might have meant
a stroke of my calf, for that, I stretch these legs to breaking,
I wrench this belly's hull, dark
as all alluvial things are. Lucifer's is a common story, a
child's boogeyman. What should frighten *you* is this:

imagine what he would be had he not fallen, had he never
known the elusive light at all, *never* been privy to the chords
of God's neck, if he, in fact, doubted such things,
believing only in what anguishes and writhes, trusting
nothing more than what soils his hands.

KEYS

The cathedral, two blocks away from a flat in a city
where I used to live, chimes every morning at dawn,
and the sound is vague, whereas the rounds fired off
on a random evening when I went back to visit were clear,
moving through the air with such clarity I stayed down flat
on the bed with an arm thrown over my still sleeping husband
until it was over—though next time a window may shatter, or
the skull of the old man a house or so over.
I found four shells the next morning in the side yard.
Sometimes the early bells toll a song I recall from a childhood
spent in a church-dotted South,
though those whitewashed churches lacked the ornament
of Saint Florian's I've come to covet.

When there is a knock on the back door, I don't answer.
Of course there are those who don't knock but try the knob
or key my car on the curb because I have a car—and
that is enough to inspire hate in someone spilling out of Kelly's
Bar next door who has saved for nothing but a week of drinks
downed in a night. Salvation works that way—a man begins to thirst
for what closed-eyed he saw glinting like mica in a stream,
and he reached from the bank of his dreams to cup that coin, to
bring it wet to the lips. I understand. I too can almost taste it:
the metal and the rapids moving through me, entering
the way the promise of bells enters. Yes. I might be saved
by such a stream if only temporarily. But consider,
the way the man that keyed my car felt momentarily assuaged
by bourbon, a drink he felt to be a drink of class to forget

he had been accused of having none, until he saw the car
daring to sit on its tires like a sign saying "You who have nothing."
He thought he was okay, thought the night had carried him to the Lethe.
I get it. But I don't blame strangers for possessing what I do not. And
I don't expect the water to be anything other than the water it is.

SKINNED

There are after all several ways to skin anything. My grandmother knew
most of those ways. She had been skinned herself (so to speak)
in that her skin was so often examined and found wanting.
What would one want to do with it really? Despite the constant oiling,
which left her arms soft as anyone could possibly desire,
her hands were ruins. She never hit me with them.
My grandfather took her with her hands at her sides.
Laundry water, cotton bolls, horse hide, the blood of goats.
She had to cook and I had to eat. She could skin a raccoon
in minutes. Revealing the purple flesh easy
as snapping a guinea neck. She would have given anything
to wake up in a new skin though hers was delightful in the light.
But what did I know?
The toil took its toll,
and though her face barely wrinkled, her knees and elbows darkened
into the skin I wear now. Roughened into the heels I scratch
against a husband's calves, because I don't listen. I refuse to wear shoes.
I'm as country as she didn't want me to be. I loved the way she smelled.
Like outdoors. Like new sheets. Like hot grease and rifle burn.
Cream of Wheat with coffee. Front porch. Corncob. Her skin
held all she did her best to scrub free. Scrubbed so hard
it liked to take the skin right off of her.
Which was what she wanted. To have it off on her own terms,
not the eyes that demonized her: *unsightly. Dirty. Unseemly.*
She saved for lace, for crinolines, for pretty gloves and
wide-brimmed hats to hide her skin. Mine is mottled. Stress blemished,
but soft as hers and I know it. Easy enough to remove. As a girl I tried
to burn it off. To find the pink I was convinced lay beneath.
I'm not the first. I wore scarves she made to cover the evidence
of my curiosity. I give myself over

to the lotions of the day. Disparage the oils she did not love
but felt she needed. She'd stroke my cheek and say "good baby,"
and I'd feel good in my skin,

in that moment.
I'd hold her tight and whisper, "You are the prettiest,"
and she'd feel good, in hers. I want to forget, but I have my mirrors.
And there she is, shadowed, in a sunstruck field.

SALT

for Veedra
(Miami, Florida)

Allergic to fish (shellfish or otherwise)
my sister shouts *Watermelon!*
when surprised by a fruit dinner
at the resort where she and I are sharing
sister time, something we rarely do.
I am old enough to be her aunt, or
even her mother. Fifteen years older
in fact, and like a mother, I take delight
in her delight. She won't be hungry
this evening, the chef has prepared
something especially for her, having
no idea what she looks like, only that
a temporary resident needs something
beyond seafood. Only the fruit is untainted.
A gentleman from Georgia sits with us
as we wait on our dinner. He, from "a good family"
"strong values" "can go back several generations"
looks at me, directly into my black pupils, and
I know what he knows. A whole history rides
the vehicle, the mule train, the wagon, the dust
track of my sister's outburst. And we begin
to laugh, hysterically. He for all the expected
reasons. And I, I laugh because somewhere
I want to cry. The landscape under my breasts,
topography of pines, clay bottomland, roofs
of tin . . . and the lie of it. The fruit so sweet, so

red, and now seedless. He and I both know
how delicious such things can be, but he can eat his
without shame, without notice.
And my sister in all her Yankee naïveté, or
innocence, knows only that she is being served
a treat, something that won't swell her throat,
noose her breath, while he and I share
our secret through grins, giggling
until we damn near choke.

EPICUREAN

A hungry mouth, an empty mouth, insistent mouth,
mouth that would be filled by the seaweed of me,
that would crack the shell with a rock and take its portion.
The mouth gauges its slide, gapes—
grotto mouth. Mouth where I might go to pray,
to fall upon my knees before. A mouth of "Yes."
Singer of heights and sorrows, Swannanoa of
a mouth. French Broad, Pigeon, a mouth still
as a North Carolina river. A mouth that keeps
its secrets like a still. Moonshine mouth of fiddles
and laments. Yes, a mouth that knows itself. Generous.
No virgin's pout, nor a greedy boy's insistence.
Give me one already schooled. Not excess
but experience.
                        Epicurus did not advocate for wine,
                        but for the salt of the skin,
and water to quench it. Paradox but not duplicity. Simple.
In my awe I would have this honest mouth, dive into the bliss
of it. Speechless mouth that makes its desires plain—

Who wouldn't want to draw the cup from this well? Give me
a mouth I might place my own chapped lips to in the heat.
A mouth to sate. A mouth to surrender.

HOW DELICIOUS TO SAY IT,

to allow it like *hibiscus* to wend over the tongue,
where it opens at the gate, lending its red, unknowable
taste. What wonder the palate may embrace—in a flick
behind the teeth: *loquacious, Liebchen, Schätzchen.*
Let us praise the labium that shapes such syllables, and
parlay of their attendant assumptions like a *shuttlecock*
struck back and forth over its simple backyard net.
Let us not neglect, but laud the mature mouth ready
for more than a *dollop*, the spoonful of *lip, loon,*
April, billow, or some simple pronoun. No. It wants *jouissance,*
Dostoevsky, provocations heating the exchange, say
chipotles in the chocolate. Consider the *uvular* awakenings
of the day, the throat stretched to signify its pleasure and release.
Your name spun through the reel, wound up from the bass
of me. How I want to say it, and hear my own, again.

for Matthew

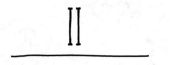

THE LEDGE

for Gregory

Not any room but this one
where everything happens
unless one is alone   He is alone   The window is barred
                                           as are most such windows
                                           in such cities
Not any room but a room
where a man alone can think himself into
laughter   remorse   feats of daring
                              Where a counter knife might become
                              a sword that frees the dragon   or
                    lops free its head
If there was a picture window
by which he could stand a passerby
might read his malaise
                         But   no such window
                         He smiles
                                   Faces the street
A bowl of cherries sits in his lap
so taut and blushed he thinks
                    to suck them clean
to leave nothing
        but a gleaming bowl
        of pits
                    A bowl of fruit and a book
                    The close world closed off
A kind of peace
                         Ruminations like children running

round and round a table until they
run out of room

He looks at the clock
A mouse runs down the hours
Over my grave

When the room is full it is full of racket
the souls of young folk
careening

He imagines heaven
as a window that might allow one
to see what one has missed

where one might
muse upon an implication
without having to   touch   it
He notes
a bonbon on the shelf   Temptation
Jesus

What can I eat?
Of sweets   "Son beware"
He considers
impatiens growing in a window box   their scent
picked up by a breeze
It is that easy to escape
to run He thinks
He runs a hand over his chest
Turning away from the shelf
like leaving a precipice
where the eye hangs
over the edge tempting
a descent
He leaves the sweet alone
for now
He has something on his mind
a memory
A shudder down the spine

Mouse over my grave
                    An old wives' tale:
                              "Hansel ate the windowsill first
                                   and as he poked
              his tongue
                        through his teeth he watched *her*
through the glazed glass
                              She
                    of the spilling pocket treats
In fact
          he fell as he watched her
and made quite a racket in the falling
Now   what kind of boy was that?
                              This ain't no tale for children
She was fat and that made her seem delicious
as she stirred and kneaded and pretended
not to watch"
                         What is a fairy tale
but a night terror
                    A torment
A story the man can't forget
                         told in its original
A pantry mouse runs down the hours
like a shiver down his spine like
the truth of a matter spilled like
cherry blossoms carpeting the rough

A memory so preciously pink
                         he fancies
the petals might bleed if pressed
         He refused that day to run to the tree
so   that day stayed pleasant enough
         The heat stayed temperate
                              suggesting a certain placidity
                              that might be taken for passion
in a certain kind of man

He tries to remember if he *ever* made love
under a cherry tree
                    That window won't open
"If there were no window Hansel would not have come through. He was
that type of boy, a boy who would not use the door. Who worked his way in
with a lick
a lock   unlocked"
                    But to be a family man
is to close the window against the weather
Against darkness   To shutter
                    To be a family man is to be alone
in the kitchen with a view of the counter
                    Hickorydickorydocked
Is to be a hero of sorts
sordid   *only* when dreaming   *or*
        in the fantasy of others
                                He has fallen
        (once or twice) asleep in his chair
and dreamt he was falling
                    Dreamt he was swallowed
Dreamt the night was a dim voice that filled him with books
                    with dust
Dreamt the books fell
                    all around him
Cried in his sleep
Reached for—
Woke and sought   a glass of milk
                current news
        the scurry of familia around his table

To be a family man is the sacrifice of family men

If there was a window through which he could be clear-
ly seen a passerby could read the hours on his face

Alone now
in this room he toasts:

> *To making bearable*
> *memories*

What does the view matter over the shoulder?

He looks forward

to company at the table
to rose-patterned plates chipped in the sink.

IMPRINT

Their concerns must be weathered
whether or not Daddy wants to wear
the duck boots and jump into puddles
as if he meant to do that silly waddle
that sets his girls giggling (and he does,
because, well, who else in all the world
would they follow with such glee?). His
dulcet darlings want only to play,
unconcerned with his concerns, the weather
being always good, *Au soleil, sous la pluie,*
he sings, and they are off—my papa
took me over a pond when I was
twenty-four, far past my childhood wiggles
but given to wandering, just like him,
we walked the wet streets mapless
and he smiled a rare smile, and we sang
the songs of childhood we'd both missed,
our feet splashing water against the brick
and cobbles. I would have followed him
anywhere, down any avenue—*l'on y danse
tous en rond*—

VISITING THE HOUSE ON LONG ISLAND

Like the memory of a monarch landing
in the palm of the hand the summer's end
contains no promise so its moment is held only briefly
Little separates this pool from the Sound
A stone wall A rail The gulls fly over both and
the gabled roofs as well Children jump into the water
as children will—headlong Oblivious to the hints
of ending
               The slight cut in the air
               Birds following the butterflies south.

CAKE BABY

(Asheville, North Carolina)

Since finding the baby in the slice
of King Cake nothing has been the same.
It's not just about me anymore. There are—
new considerations. I can't just run
around the country flying toward any dream
that takes momentary hold. Now, I am
grounded by my responsibilities. The baby
is almost translucent, with red hair and
my shape. The child I would have wanted.
Dinner out tonight will have to be canceled.
The cake baby is cold and his arms are out. To think
I almost ate him, pierced him with the fork,
to be ground under my molars. I caught my-
self in time. A visiting friend has discovered the wonder
of *patria stayputus*. He wants to wake up to his
dears every morning. What a birthday, Mardi Gras.

   And I who have never been a mother
may now proclaim myself queen with a mouthful of cake
and a baby by the side of my plate, red mouthed
and glowing as if in a fairy tale. So what the news
of the world since his birth? He is keeping me here
for a while to think things through. I think I will keep
him by the bedside. Make a crib of a small ring
box for my Tom Thumb. And when he has grown
I will ready him for a bowl of the bitter world,
lick the last of the frosting from his hair
the way a cat might bathe her own young Tom.

BREAK

The hay so pungent,
the bales tight.

The cows flick their tails.
By the field a road runs.

A city's dream when the smog is up:
of grass and bees and mother-licked calves,

of brooks and unnamed flowers.
A sun just past its apex glances down

to warm the dimming daffodils. Of course,
the expectant scampering of mice, a snake

wet as a newborn in his new skin.
Nothing to see that can't be imagined, then

the whistle. Then the bell. The small alarm
set in the phone. Then the desk, the hours ahead,

then home?

CIRCE AFTER THE FEAST OF KINE

Who doesn't have a lesser friend whispering some lie
into your ear. Just like Eurylochus, who didn't give a fuck
what Odysseus thought, he had made up his mind.
If Odysseus wouldn't hear it someone else would. You know
the type (if you're honest), half your vision but twice the hype,
and sometimes the bull gets through, and you lose the woman
you loved or the man you loved or both, point being—
there is always someone willing to take what's yours,
especially if you have more than they could possibly hold.
You hear me, don't you? The waves aren't banging the shore
too loudly are they? I wanted to make this a statement on Beauty,
how amply beauteous the bovines on the hillock near the sea,
but this is a warning, my brother. I am suggesting, dear Sojourner,
you take heed:
escape from the mast doesn't mean you won't be roped again.
But not by these sirens wide hipped as cattle, their lowing enticing
you over the ululations of the swells. No, nothing that divine.
Next time it will be the tongue of a friend whetting your ear,
someone you thought you could trust, waiting until you go
up the mountain to think, to get your head together, who will then turn
to the rest, followers all, and betray you, putting the innocent to the spit,
knowing just what it will do to you who wanted only to be liked, and
so could not see through him who wanted only to be you.

WATERFIRE

We were walking by the man-made river where a city walked
so slowly along its banks it seemed part of the current itself,
and every few feet a fire burned, the cauldron fires that smelled
of flesh, though I knew it to be only heartwood thrown
by the bare-chested men onto the flames. For a moment I forgot
where I was, and heard, a chanting. A lowing from the waters.

We followed the shore. There were kernels of corn, small explosions
in great oiled kettles being turned then poured into bags and cones.
We ate more than we needed as we talked about your future, despite
the past seeming to fill the air with smoke, I said, *In this place I imagine
civility just giving way*.

Along the man-made river, we walked, and the boats almost beside us
full of those you said "meant to be seen," but I knew otherwise as I
pictured myself weightless upon that close current, indivisible:
skin, wood, water, fire. As people waved, you went on—about Beauty
and how there simply wasn't enough of it . . .

A SONG ON THE RIDGE

I was a spinner and a speller, a seller and deceiver   back on the Ridge

I was a thief and the theft, a weaver and the weft   back on the Ridge

A tiller and a teller, a sipper and a slipper   back on the Ridge

I was the secret and the spill, a spider and the wound   back on the Ridge

I was a seer and a swiller, a quail and a hound   back on the Ridge

I heard the music and I sang it—a symphony of bark   back on the Ridge

I threw cards and the bones upon a potter's wheel   back on the Ridge

I sought shadows and the shade. I was not afraid   back on the Ridge

I was the fiddle and picker, a wife and sinner   back on the Ridge

I was lightning over water, the cross and a believer   back on the Ridge

        back on the Ridge

    back on the Ridge

      back on the Ridge

        back on the Ridge

      back on the Ridge

IV

ALL THE FUSS OVER A ROSE . . .

When Beauty was alone, she felt a great deal of compassion for poor Beast. "Alas,"
said she, "'tis thousand pities, anything so good natured should be so ugly."
—Jeanne-Marie Leprince de Beaumont, *La belle et la bête*

You would think the rose would matter more (since it always seems to matter so much what with its smell and all), but it did not. It was simply the vehicle (and there is always a vehicle) to get from point A, the Beast, to point B, the non-Beast, or from point A, a kind of power (brute strength/phallic measure) to another type of power (Beauty). Yes, it tempted the merchant, father of Beauty, and what else was he to give her? Let us be grateful he chose what he felt to be an echo, a reflection in those petals of pink instead of any other gift (which would be no gift at all, no, not at all). But he was guiltless indeed, except for the theft of the rose in the vase, which was a kinder plucking, one from which he did not escape, but his conscience, *that* was clean. In that sense, let us praise the substitute on its thin stem and those meaningless thorns (what could those hurt? It was only a single rose after all). The Beast, shall we call him that? He wouldn't mind. Or if he would, well, it's too ubiquitous a thought for him to shift an entire village's perception. So Beast it is. The power of allegory. And with that Beast, passion. Oh yes, so for those in the know (wink) being such a being has its pleasures. But who knows? Certainly not the Beauty, whose thieving father stole the blush-tinged breath of spring from the foyer. Point being C, the point of entry. Temptation led the father to steal leaving Beauty in the hands of one Beast. An exchange of sorts. Of the sordid? Well, that depends upon your perception. The way a father longs to walk a daughter down the aisle in her "beautiful" dress and give her to another like himself and feels proud to have done so, especially if her beauty is of a type to be remarked upon, if the complement of viewers on his side of the aisle can nod their heads in awed compliance. Delivery worth the dowry. And once our Beauty was in hand, the rose (only the vehicle, remember?) did what roses do in time (and this one had only hours left, its purpose having been served), it withered. Was crushed underfoot. Who cared? As for the father, he paid the price, agreeing a price should be paid for the gaze that forces the hand for Beauty. Soon stood before the

Beast the original. No copy. Beauty for the taking. And there (or not) was the rub. How to get her to rub his fur? In that spot right under the left blade? Hmm? How? How to lay her upon the bear-skinned rug, not yet christened? How to have her see his, his, potential? That's the problem with virgins, he thought (and even his thoughts were growls). As for her? How to please the Beast without paying the price? How to not be the cost?

WOLF

. . . I was a bad boy, so my daddy tol me the story bout the wolf and lil red rilin hood
—Howlin' Wolf

1
It's licking your doorknob
You know it's there
    (yesyoudo)

Sound so subtle   if not for the scent

you might pretend it's the rustle of needles
over the porch boards

you might pretend it's a coon's back up
against the pine bark

But it's there lilgirl

                that tongue like a language

all its own
And you know it
    (and you know more than that)

2
I said, *Run*   *river can't help you*
How's the river gonnahelpyou?
    All that wet pullin at you
    pullin you down into more

of itself
I was baptized like any other
Didn't do a damned thing

                      to stop me

     Just look at my mouth
I'll put it to anything
    (whatyoubet)

3
A wolf will make you faint
A wolf will have you happy

                  on your knees
and make you
           want more of the same

4
By the time we were done
I couldn't tell me from it   it from me
    Who was on the floor?
    Whowascryinglikethat?

5
Good jug
    What do you know about it?
(Nothin) (not yet)

6
By the time we finished
I knew we'd never be finished

7
When I meet the one who ain't a wolf
I'll let you know
                (maybe) (maybe I'll keep that
all to myself)
                Take a look at these teeth

8
I used to hide my pine-filled hunger
my breath of sawdust
my hardtack heels

Enough shame to splinter a belly
Enough needles to gag on
     to be fucked forever
(what the fuck are you looking at?)

9
O white-socked blue man
O foul-tongued hero

Shout down the wolf (now)
Shoot the damned thing

10
I'm a wolf, baby, and you can't believe what I say

LIGHTNIN' OVER FIR

He came to me in a dream. Train was a toy
train. Couldn't take me anywhere. Couldn't
get on. The whistle blew and I didn't answer.
He knew I wasn't going anywhere anyway.
When he pulled out his mouth harp, I said,
What you want? No way to get away.
That's how memory comes, like an incubus
over you. And you, overcome, wake up
and tell yourself it didn't mean anything.
Wake, and break your eggs into the cast iron.
Wake, and put the coffee on in a dented pot.
The next time I saw him, I'd been sleeping
for days. Waiting. In this dream I smoked
the way I used to. I drank, the way I still do.
Down the road a shack stays itself, closed
until one night it isn't. It's lit but locked.
You need the password. You have to know
how to get inside. When I pass by I hear him
playing. He's working that thing the way he does.
I'd break my knees if I weren't driving.
              When I was younger I couldn't
listen to such wolves. How could I
live and listen to that? I've got my own roads
to cross. I'm already at the station.
Someone's already playing me for keeps.

BLUSTER

. . . it is these gentle wolves who are the most dangerous ones of all.
—Charles Perrault, *Little Red Riding Hood*

I knew the path and what was on it.
I wore his favorite color. He said,
"I could just eat you up." As if I were a girl
whose cheeks he could pinch into a blush,
pluck a bit off and pop onto his tongue.
I held a rustic basket of his favorite cheeses,
a board and knife. Beneath my red coat
I wore nothing. He wore short sleeves that
made him seem hairier than if he had worn nothing.
Imbalanced somehow, the clean line of the linen,
the tufts of hair spun down his arms. Every spring
I took the path. Every spring he surprised me
with his hair-raising antics. Bucking his eyes.
Biting his lips. He'd sharpened the edges
of his teeth. He'd learned my middle name.
But ask him my favorite hue. Go on.
And he never bothered to ask how I'd been.
He had the feet of a larger wolf. He wore shoes like any
huntsman. I wanted to knock mine upon them
to test their strength. I said, *I've been away studyi—*
He said, "Don't you want to guess what I'm holding?"
I laughed because what else was there to do? I knew
his type. He was clever. Though he couldn't unsnap
my lamb's wool, he cut through it with a claw.

In the grove—so clean a slice you couldn't tell
my cape from the blood beneath it, just a circle,
a hole—I dropped my act. I smiled a heartless smile.
I arched my back and only cried a little really.
I was my grandmother's granddaughter after all.

GRASP

It starts with the glance that considers
something that has been caught
          on a line
we'd snap with our disdain
if we could have seen it, before
we realized we were being dragged to the bank.
               What a Fisher.
               The practiced fingers
that secured the hook. We would have escaped him
had he not looked down as we were looking up.
               And subtle enough
to be denied, the piercing, a needle placed
by a nurse so skilled he might be a mother blowing
on a wound, mouth by our knee before we feel the pain.
What chaos the face when gutted so. We gasp
on the shore of it, our skin chafed by the sand of it,
our chambers ruptured on its rocks.
Before the inevitable we attempt to hold ourselves in,
but out everything spills. Then, in a fish eye, the Fisher
sees the depths (whose hints he'd ignored) shadowing his
own the way trees shadow a watercolor lake.

SEEN THROUGH

Such thin things—a white shirtsleeve,
the glancing eye lighting upon the glancing
eye, the smell of soap on the skin
before the sun heats everything to discomforting
sharpness. The barriers are so permeable really—
a membrane, simple and opaque between knowing
and knowing better. I don't stroke your back,
don't reach to heal the fragile vertebrae
beneath the porous cotton starched into an envelope,
like an invitation, I don't dare open.

V

PARADISE

(Crockett, Texas)

In the pines
in the pines
where the sun don't ever shine
I would shiver the whole night through.
                    —Leadbelly

Don't tell me, I was there. And the songs
are mine who slept there, who dreaded the shade
of the trees at dusk, their mountain silhouette.
I feared and was without shame in my fright.
Who wouldn't turn from that darkness?
I was told to walk the property line. I was told
to hold the pistol. I climbed my grandpa's feet
to sit on his wide lap, my head on his barreled chest.
A beggar for stories to counter such dusk.
Taller than the pines. The men that marked those pines
in red were slim as the pines themselves. They stood apart
and hated us but loved our music, our rough-spun bodies
for the having (then). Unless your own clan molders
beneath those mounds, you don't know, and
you can believe me or not.

TINTYPE

(Thunderstorm in Palestine, Texas, 3:00 P.M.)

Tin roof, ten teeth, three gold, as if from a tin pan
in a slow creek drawing mud, calling up catfish
from the muck, and that skinny man, Aunt Tinny's
man, never married, married man. He's got his
head thrown back. Eyes closed for his daily claim:
the way she pulls the hurt right out
of him, like a long splinter whose release
almost feels good. Real good.
He cooks but doesn't eat. Doesn't need
anything but what he took years back
and keeps shacked in front of him. A woman
tinned her own cans back there, back then,
and burned trash in the backyard. You think I don't
know who I am? Tin tonguing the gap
between there—listening with my hands stuck
to my chest and the ring shout of my own feet—
and now. "Tin cutter. Just like me," to hear Tinny
tell it. Once you've sat on that sweat-stained couch,
pot-liquor spotted, love-marked cushions
frayed to failing, and listened to her pound
the upright's keys, some tan, and half-rotted
black. Barely standing, and the bench barely able
to hold her tin-haired self, you won't be right.
She'll mess you up if you stay too long, tin man.
That wail wrapping its arms around you, its legs
like a weighted trap. You'll cry for your mother.
You'll cry like you've never cried before.

'Course you will. Taking in what can't be
taken in. Won't matter who you were,
she'll give it to you anyway, your heart rolled
in her mouth, ten times the measure, over days
like one long road of night, cold, hard as hail.

SHE WHOSE BROTHERS TURNED TO SWANS PLEADS HER CASE

The first word you utter will pierce through the hearts of your brothers . . . Their lives hang upon your tongue.
　　　　—Hans Christian Andersen, *The Wild Swans*

You'll find no swans here. No wet feather bed. Did you think
upon this shadowed lake
you would? Floating on their white bellies of
down and
such common dreams I could pluck them from the air, sweet
graveling
as spray rising from foam, from the spittle and
the spite of bonbon stuffed dolls—your Trumpeters. Cloy of not chocolate
but of the tempting runoff, the opaque butterfat, what flies off the dark left
behind. But you, you can be sated only by what rots you. To
be clearer: these waters yield no treasures you'd seek. Folly
cold whipped below
finds me, however, opening like a dead pirate's trove or
the ribcage of a lesser bird, a woolen albatross
dunked and forgotten, hastily buried, aching to float up, to
be magically cut from this anchor: the weight of your loss, and my fate.

STILL LIFE WITH DEAD GAME

Chumps prefer a beautiful lie to an ugly truth.
                    —Iceberg Slim

But I'm speaking of what the body keeps inside,

when the eyes are a window to nothing,
                                                    a woman

alone in a room, pretty music in her ugly head.

Not eighteenth century. Still, she's cultured enough,
her feathered skirt   hangs perfectly,

a sixteenth-century still life.
Touch her. *It wouldn't take much to take her*

                                                    there.

I'm describing the body tethered between worlds.   Framed
into her posture.   Illustration:
I'm speaking of what clothes hide.   Clothes?

She wears them thin. She's worn-out
holding up the cutout.   Underneath

She's unraveled, but pull the thread.

                                                    What do you think?

She won't dignify your fingering with a response.   So composed.
Take an X-Acto knife to the canvas. Go ahead, brother.

                                                    She won't flinch.

I won't get blood on the floor.

THE OLD MASTER

His heart was miserably small and
toward the end it was his heart that caved upon itself,
the thinning walls collapsed into the hollow.
The weight upon it broke it: questions of existence,
memories of his mother. He had seen the end
coming. In the last year of his final marriage
he dreamed he was a woman without means.
A tumbled woman. He felt he had been such
a woman in a previous life, a dour witch
pressed for harming her neighbors through charm,
through craft. She had gazed too long upon a stable boy.
She had looked directly into the eyes of her betters.
She had eaten parsnips straight from the ground.
She had been seen squatting in the rows. They said,
She must know the Beast, so shameless. He had refused
goodly company and talk. He had come to understand
with his own limitation those with even smaller hearts.
He noted how luminous the eyes of the envious
when the end came, as his own weight felled him.

ON THE LAST DAY

considering Miłosz

No one will taste the bread in their mouths.

A dying man will break his ribs falling from a ledge.
Others will follow him over. Of course.
A plane, unable to land in the valley for the winds,
will keep flying until it doesn't. No one will look up.
Why look up now?
No one will be prepared, so there will be no Thanksgivings.
But they *will* know.
On the last day, *Why?* will tear the eyes so
no one will notice the grass or the flowers
or the badger or the bear at the trash cans.
A stroller will roll down the road.
At last the day's fashions will stop turning the days.
Those who held hands will hold hands.
Those who kissed the day before will kiss again
and mean it. Those with love will have it.
Those without will go without. Did you think it would be
otherwise? Those who were wronged will not be righted.
Those without empathy have already perished.
Oblivious. Those who sought fairness will find
only equanimity. Monsters will feast upon Beauty
as they have always done. And all the thin sibyls will
topple from their platforms. But you, my friend?
You will remain exactly where you are.

INEVITABILITY

There is always a cage at the center, a lockup,
the place you may wind up no matter
how hard you try to follow the straight and
narrow, there's a jailer with a key and no occasion
prevents the key's jangling. The boys at a game in Philly,
let's say, know a few beers could get them put in
that cell, the one kept for the rowdy, the rude,
those whose parameters were long ago
shot to hell by a lonely mother, the boys who step out
of line, who won't acknowledge the fucking line.
Without having laid eyes on the place (you know
the place) you know there's a dried mattress
and a Styrofoam cup of tepid water. Taste it?
Notice the smell? You'll worry it's you,
while above your head, the you you were before
is quoting the score and taking life in gulps,
anxious inside because you knew you
would end up here. You, who never could just
walk away from a too-good thing. You
with something to prove, a drama unfolding
like a thin blanket barely covering the frame.

ONE TO ANOTHER

It's like a spirit from some dark valley . . .
      —Howlin' Wolf

that hard loll of tongue again like a bent straight razor roving up
then down the neck   of that sweet thing *letting herself go that way* . . .

and you not giving a damn 'cause you're hungry 'cause your nose was open
and you got a whiff of her long before you knew what to do with her and

I'd blame you but I've got my own obsessions I've got my own
instrument meant to draw down the moan   and these licks   well   I'd

say we are kindred   you and I on all fours   or two
each holding on to that thing we need any way we can   just

to keep it all together under skin that threatens to split then
there'd we be   bare under a moon white enough for us

to see who we really are and just what we've done.

APOLOGIA

*In short, everything succeeded so well that the youngest daughter began to think
that the man's beard was not so very blue after all, and that he was a mighty
civil gentleman.*
—Charles Perrault, *Blue Beard*

As you asked me not to open the door
I shouldn't have—
but what are shoulds? Should I have touched
your face that first night? Overcome
with curiosity, my fear was your blue beard
between my legs—
a nightmare I couldn't shake,
and now must receive, the feather of it,
each hair's nightly collapse against my own
webbing.

When you left, I went to your swan's coop,
snapped every slender neck
in the lot. Then the other fowl, those bewildered
chicks puffing and pecking aimlessly at their own
scatter never looked up.

How angry I was, to have a key I couldn't use.
I cut my locks so you would have nothing to take
hold of, loosed then lifted each curl
with your gold scissors. How the high marks the low.

I explored every room save *that* one—

moving from treasure to treasure naked as the night,
sought you out object to object, lair by lair,
sat on every divan, scratched my head
against every pillow.

So after months without, I gave way,
pulled the key from my small purse and found them there,
all of them, like birds brined and preserved on drying hooks,
their black cloaks so stiff against the brick,

I did not scream. I thought—*stupid starlings*—

A cool salt draft kept the blood-soaked floor
as sand might, so I did not slip,
not then.
From the window I considered the fall, but
I was so pleased to be alive, to realize I now had you,
if only briefly, all to myself. Dear blade,
so what the truncated future? It is the licks I know
are coming that will buckle and betray me.

NIGHTJAR

Its flight was soundless, the wings full of air.
The feathers. The feathers. I didn't imagine this.
I opened my eyes and there above me it hovered,
as if considering what should happen next.
I was not yet asleep. It was dusk. But I had worked
since dawn and needed to rest. Let myself collapse
upon the bed. Had I opened a window?
It seemed to float. I could feel the rapidity
of its heart. It stared as if it did not know it was staring.
Not wanting to frighten it I did not reach, though
I wanted to. It remained just inches away. Reluctant incubus.
Crepuscular darling. How could I fear it? So urgent—
my muscles relaxed as I concentrated
all of my attention on the intruder—so hesitant.
I mouthed, *Lower*. I lay still as an invitation.

HER MOUTH

"We could not bury her in the dark ground," and they had a transparent coffin of glass
made, so that she could be seen from all sides, and they laid her in it . . .
     —The Brothers Grimm, *Schneewittchen*

A spider came and went
A bit of October leaf lodged
in the left corner
Her lips chapped and faded
What a nest above her brow?
Who had done her hair?
Undone her corset?
Who left her shoeless?
Skirt above her knees
Hem unraveling
No one kissed her
All prodded
Pinched
What trauma, dreams
Someone tried to feed her
Someone fingered out a bit
of roughage
Her eyes were parted
as were her lips
A spliced heart
One
Prince
dared
look
down
that

throat
Took in her soured breath
Another spider
Another
Another
Another Prince deigned bend
to place a hand upon her
ruddy cheek
A maid's profile
Found her frigid there beneath
the juniper
Then snowfall
Then rain
Then
Then
On the days went
No one kissed that mouth of webs
still so prettily shaped
for the taking.

CONSIDER THE PRINCE AS HE CONSIDERED HER MOUTH

He saw the coffin on the mountain, and the beautiful Snow-white within it . . .
—The Brothers Grimm, *Schneewittchen*

Consider the Prince dying alone. No,
that can't be considered. Then, consider the Kingdom,
its future, think of the Crown's weight as
the Prince becomes King of all he surveys.
          Having left his love to the snow
of her own desires. Consider the way he dotes
upon the Queen he finally finds, the one who meets
most of his expectations, not a Virgin but close enough,
cool to the touch, placid rider blushing her ruby nipples
with a pitted cherry. Note: a proper consummation with
bloodstained sheet (no matter how), and how laughter
now rings around the Hall, children bright and toothsome
as ponies. Consider lineage and a father's Majesty in joy:
Well met son, well met. Consider the Prince's (now King's)
dreams, the forest alive as a lilting voice, as a song sung
into the ear. He feels the lips just brush his right lobe,
such a lovely melody it cleaves his heart. Consider
his waking and his consternation upon waking, knowing
he cannot stop dreaming of those mountains, the silhouettes
of Linden dark against a darker sky. The open casket
where she lives and will never die, but will remember the *no*
he whispered. The mouth that did not meet hers. Judicator.
Consider, the body he could not touch without wincing,
the beauty denied under that raven's nest of hair, her lips
blued by cold, and that dirty smock
upon which seven sets of smudged fingerprints rested,
for all the world to see.

HAVING NEVER TOLD THE TAROT READER MY QUESTION, SHE ANSWERS IT

The old woman's hands fast-forward two cards by two
without pause except for the questions she asks,
which I won't answer, she being the reader,
                                        let her tell me.
And there sits the penultimate card: OPPRESSION:
two black arms wrapped awkwardly around two black arms,
in love or in conflict, either way, burdened. Dysmorphia is
the term I've come to live with in the mirror, not my face
but in my face's stead the marks of childhood, remarks,
hardened like a mask of papier-mâché into place. Monster,
gorilla, sundry beasts—and the adults with their droll faces,
their insider nods, *Kids will be kids*.
                      I stood before them and they looked askance,
drew their conclusions, drew down their
mouths. And if I were to leave my cave of reckonings? What
arrow might explode my scaled neck? this hide? wreck these
ruins so perfectly set, like the forty-ninth bullet in a dead horse's
side. It was the final card, BEAUTY, from which rose the wings
of a swan, swaddled in the expected white clouds that made me
believe. I caught that reader's eyes just then and saw reflected
your face in all its impassive judgment.

GUTTED

We've spoken of that fish before. The one that sought
the hook and then the eye of the fisherman. We wondered,
What kind of fish was that? Thinking so much
of itself. Refusing to gasp on the boards but
staring up as if to say it was more than what it seemed
to be. In the end it was sliced like any other
fish. Riven tail to head. That's right. *Fucking fish.*
Into the frying pan. Into a gullet. But
the fish stays on the mind somehow. *Can't forget,*
the fisherman muses. Until it's all he thinks about,
the fish and its wet eye. Its tremulousness.
The fish and the way it slipped from his hands,
how he kept reaching for it. How
it refused to gasp against the board. It stared
up as if to say, we are more than what we seem.
Some days the fisherman's fillet knife slips. He cuts
a thumb, or the inside of his thigh while sitting in
the boat. Can't keep his mind on the task at hand.
Just a fish, and this thought comforts for a time.

BLACK RIVER

She thought to throw herself in, to
take to the water what had been released,
unraveled, swirled about her like hair
in high wind, like the current in spring,
season of beginnings, she thinks, as she tucks up
her cotton dress, the white one.

That she had held something like that
within for so long was a wonder to her,
though she was no simple woman (despite
her bare feet and their indiscretion).
She had a mind to become someone acceptable,
a woman who did not draw on her arms,
a woman who did not jump as a girl would,
so many ways to disappoint, to wear down
the surrounding world. She means to surrender
to the rippling. Why not? The water
bracing in the cold melt.

Now that she no longer carried what had held her
for so long, nor cared who knew, she says to no one
in particular, *Let the river carry me like a shell
to unknown waters, let me be filled with another
spirit, this time, one that will see and abide.*

JOIN

Here you are my tin surgeon,
on your beauteous knees, eyeing this mystery
with such distress: again, the belly's suture re-
opened. Too much weight placed upon the wall
of muscle and nerves run under the surface.
Then the expected spilling, though this time
less the egress of an eruption than the intermittent
evincing of steam from a street's metal aperture.
This is how my liver came through, and my heart,
plopped without dignity from the vent
just before my spleen (ridiculous filter).
                    I bent to capture what
I thought I needed, to gather within my arms
what I could not seem to keep together, but
there is magic in the world, and the seam
began to mend. Invisible clamps closed
the flesh tight as a virgin's lips (though
the evidence of my healing is not at all pretty,
nothing to desire). But if you really want to see—
I'll show you. There's nothing. Not a gurgle,
nor a swoosh of blood through gray tributaries.
Hollow. Yet here I stand, composed as Frankenstein's
Monster, as one with everything intact.

VI

FLYING OVER PIGEON RIVER

I think of "home" and The way we find our way back

Despite the winds that threaten The wings And

there's the daunting lope of every damned thing

More than once the gully found me More than that

I've slid Lost my footing Ugly bird Couldn't stand

Flight was a fool's notion and with it I have grown

Tenacious and scabrous I have suffered the fall

and again But I love best the nest Where you wait

and I   land.

ALL KINDS OF HOWLIN'

Wolf is just one There's the wind
between houses Cold as a tongue
in a *couldn't care less* mouth There's
that belt or hand whistling through air to meet
a backside and The cry a woman makes
when she meets her Maker
                          Wolf is just one
way to get there To that pain that rocks
your bones Rocking away

BEAST AND BEAUTY

He took me like a mother, drew my head toward himself,
pulled me onto his lap, wrapped his arms around me and cooed
into my hair, softly as if I was dreaming and
                                    he didn't want to wake me.
He sang a song that sounded like *birds singing in the sycamore*
then tree frogs. I wanted to leave. I stayed where I was.
He wore a lovely shirt. His hair was surprisingly kempt.
There was half a candle piece and a rug of quarters. Tomato soup
on the stove. I thought, "What a shirt." I prayed my breasts
would magically spill from the zipper. I wanted to feel my calloused heels
on his thighs. I wanted *to linger 'til dawn*. His pared nails scratched
an itch that had eluded me for years. I cried as if I were slicing onions
in his kitchen. He was a good mother. He held me, like a daughter,
as if I was just as beautiful, as he believed me to be.

HUSBAND FAIR

for Matthew

How good to lay with my husband in our stone flat, though
there are not enough windows and too many doors. We need another
chair. Smaller tables wobble too much for books and won't
hold both of our plates. But we eat, he and I, and the fare's good.
I cook simply because he doesn't know how. Never learned.
I don't mind. The food is mine too. He cooks and we laugh. How good
to tell him "no" when I feel like it, and "yes" and "maybe,"
and we laugh more, so freeing, he and I, so freely, though
not carefree—
there are bill collectors
that threaten, and the roof over our heads, over our small bed,
is not one we own. We own so little, but we get by, we go
from here to there to here, on need and on whim, for desire,
for work. How different from my line, from that woman
not so distant, who never went anywhere beyond a field of bolls,
who lay with another's husband, my grandfather not so many father's ago.
He who owned so very much and her, pinned beneath him, his arms of rope,
his body of winter, who laughed only when she cried, his face a heavy drift
over hers, her face brown as earth below, brown as my own.

A SMALL POEM

for Jen Chang and Martha

From a morning without expectations a surprise,
a word unanticipated and meant. Rare
and jarring. Syllables moving one to tears
when the winter sky is a simple blue, and nothing
is there to impede the dailyness of things. But
the word grows from a note a hello a salutation
and plants itself like a spring dandelion seed that by
afternoon is full grown and blowing more seeds,
lightly, sweetly, a coloratura of delight, and I
feel as if I were both the plucked and the child
plucking the stem and twirling. How a single word
can set the world turning from one moment into
the next in startlement.

CHIMERA

She's not "maternal," she's dangerous.
—Jamaal May

I have no charms. Admittedly.
No gold comb can move through
This mane. My skin is not translucent.
Mine is a tail to fear. I know.
And though a mother may destroy,
She too sees fit to create beauty
That would eventually grow into forms
I would swallow if I gave in
To my hungers. Nothing will come
Of this womb. But, up from my wounds—
From this goat's body—
Up from my wood-smoke lungs, from
The milk of me, comes a song, a melody
To open yours, then lick them clean.